Project

Dinosaur

Steve Parker

Miles
Kelly

First published in 2015 by Miles Kelly Publishing Ltd
Harding's Barn, Bardfield End Green, Thaxted, Essex, CM6 3PX, UK

Copyright © Miles Kelly Publishing Ltd 2015

This edition printed 2018

2 4 6 8 10 9 7 5 3 1

Publishing Director Belinda Gallagher
Creative Director Jo Cowan
Editorial Director Rosie Neave
Designers Joe Jones, Andrea Slane
Projects Author Gillian Chapman
Indexer Jane Parker
Image Manager Liberty Newton
Production Elizabeth Collins, Caroline Kelly
Reprographics Stephan Davis, Jennifer Cozens, Thom Allaway
Assets Lorraine King

ISBN 978-1-78617-528-1

Printed in China

British Library Cataloguing-in-Publication Data
A catalogue record for this book is available from the British Library

Made with paper from a sustainable forest

www.mileskelly.net

How to use the projects

This book is packed full of amazing facts about dinosaurs. There are also 11 cool projects, designed to make the subject come alive.

Before you start a project:

● Always ask an adult to help you.

● Read the instructions carefully.

● Gather all the supplies you need.

● Clear a surface to work on and cover it with newspaper.

● Wear an apron or old t-shirt to protect your clothing.

Notes for helpers:

● Children will need supervision for the projects, usually because they require the use of scissors, or preparation beforehand.

● Read the instructions together before starting and help to gather the equipment.

IMPORTANT NOTICE

The publisher and author cannot be held responsible for any injuries, damage or loss resulting from the use or misuse of any of the information in this book.

SAFETY FIRST!

Be careful when using glue or anything sharp, such as scissors.

How to use
If your project doesn't work the first time, try again — just have fun!

Supplies
The equipment should be easy to find, around the house or from a craft store. Always ask before using materials from home.

Numbered stages
Some stages of the project are numbered and illustrated. Follow the stages in the order shown to complete the project. If glue or paint is used, make sure it is dry before moving onto the next stage.

T rex puppet!

Make a *T rex* snarl and bite to show off his teeth!

SUPPLIES
pencil ● A4 white card ● tracing paper ● colouring pencils or felt-tip pens ● scissors ● three split pins ● two wooden dowels about 30 cm long ● sticky tape

1. Copy the picture of the *T rex* adult on this page to A4 size.

2. Trace the *T rex* outline without the back legs and lower jaw. Transfer onto card, colour in and cut out.

3. Trace the outlines of the back legs and lower jaw and transfer them onto the card. Add a 3 cm tab where each piece will attach to the body. Colour in and cut out.

4. Attach the back legs to the body and the jaw to the neck with split pins, making sure the pieces move freely.

5. Tape the dowels to the back of the body and the lower jaw.

HOW TO USE
T rex is supported by the dowel attached to the body. The other dowel moves the jaw up and down. The legs will move when you shake the puppet!

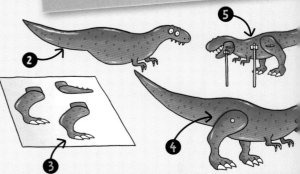

CONTENTS

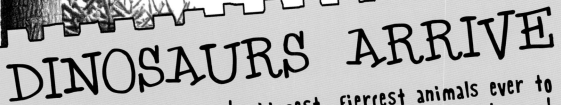

DINOSAURS ARRIVE

Dinosaurs were among the biggest, fiercest animals ever to walk the Earth. Some were giant plant-chewers, larger than a house. Others were mini bug-munchers, smaller than a pet cat. The first dinosaurs lived over 230 million years ago, and they ruled the land for more than 170 million years.

VICTORINO DINO

One of the first dinosaurs was *Herrerasaurus*, which lived in Argentina, South America, about 231 million years ago. It was about 3 m long including its tail, ran fast on its two back legs, and chased small creatures to eat. *Herrerasaurus* is named after local farmer and part-time fossil-hunter Victorino Herrera, who found its remains in 1959.

▼ Dinosaurs had straight legs positioned directly under the body, unlike the bent, sprawling legs of reptiles such as crocodiles. This positioning allowed dinosaurs to run quickly.

Plateosaurus

Silesaurus, a close relative of dinosaurs

Herrerasaurus

The first dinos

Dinosaurs appeared during the Triassic Period, 252–201 million years ago (mya). They first appeared in South America, then spread to North America, Europe, Africa and around the world.

Dinosaurs are small but grow, evolve and spread

Dinosaurs become larger especially in North America

The biggest-ever dinosaurs live in South America and Africa

Great dinosaurs have died out but some survive – as birds

Birds spread all around the world to every continent

Avian dinosa live on – we them bird

| TRIASSIC 252–201 mya | JURASSIC 201–145 mya | CRETACEOUS 145–66 mya | PALEOGENE 66–23 mya | NEOGENE 23–2.6 mya | QUATERN. 2.6 mya– |

SMALL AND SPEEDY

About 200 million years ago *Coelophysis* lived in North America. Around 2.5 metres in length, it was slim and speedy, with a long bendy neck and whippy tail. Its small, sharp, curved teeth show that it ate bugs, worms, small reptiles and similar animals, which it grabbed with its hands and clawed fingers.

▼ *Coelophysis* had big eyes and could see well. In its mouth were about 50 pointed, back-curved teeth. It may have moved around in groups.

Long tail

Long neck

Long muscular legs

DEATH AT GHOST RANCH

In 1947, over 1000 fossils of *Coelophysis* were found at a place called Ghost Ranch, New Mexico, USA. It seems they all died together. Maybe they were travelling and feeding in a group that was swept away by a sudden flood, and drowned together in a big heap.

Supercontinent!

Make a world map where the continents move – just like the real ones. Through time, the continents have drifted around the globe at 2–4 cm per year. At the start of the Dinosaur Age, they were all joined together into one supercontinent, Pangaea. This was surrounded by a superocean, Panthalassa.

SUPPLIES

map at the back of this book • tracing paper and pencil • A4 green card and white card • scissors • black felt pen • small self-adhesive magnets • old metal (baking) tray • blue acrylic paint • paintbrush

Over millions of years, Pangaea broke apart into separate landmasses. You can see the rough shapes of today's continents below. India is classed as a subcontinent – today it is part of Asia.

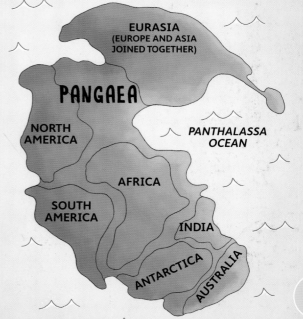

EURASIA (EUROPE AND ASIA JOINED TOGETHER)

PANGAEA

NORTH AMERICA

PANTHALASSA OCEAN

AFRICA

SOUTH AMERICA

INDIA

ANTARCTICA

AUSTRALIA

GETTING BIGGER

As time passes, all living things change or evolve. Dinosaurs did too. They spread and evolved into new and different kinds, many much bigger than the early dinosaurs. Some took to eating plants while others became strong, fast, fierce hunters.

Plateosaurus

Eustreptospondylus

GIANT JAWS

A fearsome carnivore (meat-eater), *Eustreptospondylus* prowled England 165 million years ago. Up to 6 m long, it had a large head with strong jaws to attack and tear up victims. Some fossils show it may have hunted along the shore for fish and other water creatures.

LONG NECK

Plateosaurus chewed plants about 210 million years ago in Europe. It was one of the first really big dinosaurs, at 10 m in length and a weight of 4 tonnes. Its long neck allowed it to reach far around or even up into trees to gather leaves and similar foods.

LUMPY BACK

Around 4 m long and weighing 300 kg, small-headed *Scelidosaurus* was a tough-looking herbivore (plant-eater). It plodded around the British Isles 190 million years ago. The ridged bony lumps called scutes along its back, sides, legs and tail, protected it against attacks by predatory dinosaurs.

Scelidosaurus

Cookie monsters!

Sauropods needed to feed for many hours each day to survive! These delicious dinosaur cookies will be eaten up fast by all your friends – so make plenty! This recipe makes about 24 cookies.

SUPPLIES

225g butter (softened) • 110g caster sugar • 1 egg yolk 2 tsp vanilla extract • 275g plain flour • large bowl • wooden spoon • sieve • non-stick baking tray • small plastic dinosaur toys • pre-heated oven at 170°C • cooling rack Some adult help to use the oven

HOW TO MAKE

1. Cream the butter and sugar together in the bowl using the wooden spoon until light and fluffy. Beat in the egg yolk and the vanilla extract.

2. Sift in the flour and stir well. You may need to work the dough with your hands to give it a really good mix!

3. Roll 3-cm balls of dough in your hands and place on the baking tray, flattening them slightly to make cookie-shaped.

4. Press the plastic dinosaurs into each cookie to make different impressions.

5. Bake in the oven for 12–15 minutes or until golden brown. Place them on a rack to cool before eating.

Make sure the plastic dinosaurs are spotlessly clean before pressing them into the cookies! Just use the head or footprints of larger toys to make impressions in the cookies.

◄ The legs of *Diplodocus* were strong and long. These giants often had to travel to find new food.

Spreading out

ne second part of the Mesozoic Era called the Jurassic Period. This sted from 201–145 million years ago.

Move the continents on your world map (p5) to their position during the end of the Jurassic Period (above). Most are still close together, allowing land animals to spread easily.

RIASSIC	JURASSIC	CRETACEOUS	PALEOGENE	NEOGENE	QUATERNARY
–201 mya	201–145 mya	145–66 mya	66–23 mya	23–2.6 mya	2.6 mya–now

FEATHERS, FLUFF, FUZZ

Fossil-hunters have now found many kinds of dinosaurs with coverings of feathers. Some had flight feathers like those on a bird's wings. Some had soft fluff, like a bird's down feathers. Some had fuzzy hair-like strands. And some dinosaurs had all three kinds!

Filament-like feathers on hips and tail

BIGGEST WITH FEATHERS

Yutyrannus was a huge hunter from China around 124 million years ago. A relative of the great *Tyrannosaurus*, it was not much smaller – 9 m long and 1.5 tonnes in weight. It is the biggest dinosaur known with feathers. These were up to 20 cm long and strand- or thread-like.

Powerful back legs with three-toed feet

Large toe claws

TWO-LEGGED RUNNER

Microraptor was a small meat-eater, just 75 cm long, from China 120 million years ago. It had feathers all over its body, from head to tail – even its back legs. This made running on the ground awkward. But in the air...

► *Yutyrannus* had a narrow bony crest sticking up along the middle of its snout, and a strange outward-pointing, bony 'horn' near each eye.

Long strand-like feathers on neck

50-plus sharp teeth

Tiny arms

SMALLEST WITH FEATHERS

One of the smallest feathery dinosaurs was *Mei*, at just 50 cm long. It had feathers on its head, body, legs and bony tail, and its teeth were small, sharp and close-set for eating small creatures. It was preserved with its head tucked under one arm – like a sleeping bird.

Feathery timeline

New feathered or fluffy dinosaurs are discovered almost every year.

1861: First fossils of the feathery bird *Archaeopteryx*

1998: Peacock-like *Caudipteryx*

1999: Scythe-claw *Beipiaosaurus*

Micro-glider

Make your own flying feathered *Microraptor* and see if it can glide.

SUPPLIES

strips of thick card 50 cm x 5 cm, 30 cm x 5 cm, 20 cm x 5 cm • 4 elastic bands • sheets of coloured paper • scissors • glue stick • coloured pencils/felt-tip pens

HOW TO MAKE

1. Place the two smaller strips across the longer body strip to make the body and four wings. Criss-cross two elastic bands at each junction point to secure the wings with the longer pair near the head.

2. Cut lots of feather shapes from the coloured paper and glue them along the wings, overlapping slightly. Put the same number on each side of each pair of wings for balance. Glue feathers to the tail end.

3. Cut the head of the glider into a point to make the beak. Add the eyes and colour the rest of the body.

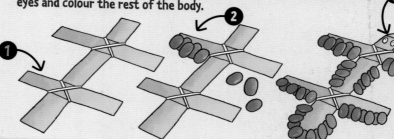

HOW TO USE

Hold the Micro-glider about 1 m off the ground and gently throw it forward. If it nose-dives, move the back wings towards the tail. If it rises and then crashes, move them slightly forwards. If it doesn't glide, turn it into a Micro-mobile!

FAMILY LIFE

Most reptiles today breed by laying eggs, which hatch into babies. Dinosaurs, which were also reptiles, did the same. Fossils show that some dinosaurs made nests for their eggs, looked after them as they developed, and even brought food for their babies!

GOOD MOTHERS

Maiasaura was a plant-eater about 7 m long that lived 77 million years ago in North America. Its name means 'good mother lizard'. Fossils of hundreds of adults, nests, eggs, babies and young show that many *Maiasaura* raised their families in one area, called a breeding colony.

How old?

Some dinosaur fossils have rings in the bones, like trees have in their trunks. Using these and other clues, experts can estimate their lifespans.

Small dinosaurs: 5–7 years

Medium-sized dinosaurs: 10–20 years

Big meat-eaters: 30–40 years

Medium-large: plant-eaters 20–30 years

Horned and armoured dinosaurs: 30–50 years

Giant plant-eaters: 70–100 years

▼ Each *Maiasaura* parent made a nest that was far enough from others in the breeding group, or colony, so the eggs did not get trodden on or stolen.

Each nest was a scoop of earth hollowed out with a raised rim, containing up to 40 eggs

BENDY SHELL

Maiasaura eggs were about 20 cm long. The shell was not hard, like a bird's egg, but tough and bendy, like thin leather. It allowed in vital oxygen from the air for the baby inside.

The parent covered the eggs with old plants, which gave off heat as they rotted to keep the eggs warm

ggs and nest

Make a nest of dino eggs and look after them until they hatch!

SUPPLIES

balloons ● small plastic dinosaur toys ● newspaper ● PVA and glue brush ● acrylic paints for decoration and paintbrush sheets of green and brown sugar paper ● scissors

HOW TO MAKE

1. Stretch the neck of a balloon open and carefully put a small dinosaur toy inside. Blow up the balloon and knot the end.

2. Tear sheets of newspaper into strips and cover the balloon with two layers using the glue. Make sure you don't cover the knotted end of the balloon. Leave to dry. Make as many eggs as you like!

3. Once dry, holding onto the knot, pop the balloon and pull it out from the inside of the egg. Cover over the hole with pieces of glued newspaper. Leave to dry.

4. Once dry, paint the eggs. Use any colour you like as no one knows what colour dinosaur eggs were.

5. Scrunch up pieces of coloured sugar paper to make a nest for the eggs. Cut out paper leaf shapes to cover the eggs.

HOW TO USE

Listen to the baby dinosaurs moving inside their eggs when you shake them – when you think they are ready to hatch, break open the shells.

WELL-FED BABIES

The newly hatched babies were 40 cm long. Their bones were not strong enough for them to walk or run. However their teeth had signs of wear from eating. This could mean the parents brought food to them in the nest.

DINO GANG

Psittacosaurus, was a small parrot-beaked plant-eating dinosaur that lived in East Asia 120 million years ago. One amazing set of fossils shows a group of about 30 young *Psittacosaurus* that died together, perhaps when a cave they were sheltering in collapsed.

The nests were 5–7 m apart, enough room for parents to walk between them

SEAS AND SKIES

During the Dinosaur Age, other great creatures flew high in the sky and swam in the sea. Like the dinosaurs, these creatures were reptiles. Some were as huge and fearsome as the dinosaurs themselves.

RHAMPHORHYNCHUS
This long-tailed pterosaur was a winged reptile, and the wings were thin skin stretched between very long finger bones. Its long, thin, sharp teeth probably grabbed fish from the water.

Size: Wingspan 1.8 m
Time: 150 million years ago
Place: British Isles

ELASMOSAURUS
A type of sea reptile called a plesiosaur, Elasmosaurus had long, sharp teeth that it probably used to spear fish and squid. Almost half of its total body length was made up by its neck, which probably wasn't particularly flexible.

Length: 14 m
Time: 80 million years ago
Place: North America

LIOPLEURODON
With four big paddle-shaped limbs, Liopleurodon was a fast, sleek swimmer. Its massive mouth and pointed fangs probably tore apart large victims such as ichthyosaurs and big fish.

Length: 7 m
Time: 150 million years ago
Place: Europe

14

Too cool!

The biggest flying animal of all time was the pterosaur *Quetzalcoatlus* from 70 million years ago. With a nose-to-tail length of 9 m, its wings spanned 11 m – three times more than today's longest-winged bird, the albatross.

The biggest sea reptile of all time was *Shastasaurus*, from the ichthyosaur group, 210 million years ago. At 20 m long, it was almost as huge as today's great whales. It probably ate small fish and squid.

PTERANODON

Pteranodon was one of the biggest short-tailed pterosaurs. It had a long beak, no teeth, and a tall pointed bony crest. It probably soared over the sea, snatching fish and similar creatures.

Size: Wingspan 6 m
Time: 85 million years ago
Place: North America

ARCHAEOPTERYX

The earliest known true bird was Archaeopteryx. Unlike modern birds it had teeth, claws on its wings and a long bony tail. But its wings and feathers were designed for proper flight.

Size: Wingspan 60 cm
Time: 150 million years ago
Place: Germany

MOSASAURUS

This huge reptile was a close relative of today's monitor lizards. Its flipper-limbs were quite small so it probably powered through the ocean by swishing its long tail from side to side, hunting all kinds of prey.

Length: 17 m
Time: 85 million years ago
Place: North America

15

HORNS AND ARMOUR

Two groups of dinosaurs were far from being fast and agile. Instead they were big, slow, heavy and well protected. They were the ceratopsians or horn-faced dinosaurs, and the armoured ankylosaurs – dinosaur versions of today's armadillos and rhinos.

Body and tail covered in lumps and spikes of bone amour

SPIKES AND LUMPS

Edmontonia lived 70 million years ago in North America, and grew to a length of 7 m. It had hard lumps of bone on its head, back and tail, with rows of spikes along its neck and sides. Its low head meant it could eat only plants at ground level.

Scary horn-face mask

Make a *Triceratops* mask and scare your friends!

SUPPLIES
paper and pencil • big board or tray • plasticine-type modelling material • petroleum jelly newspaper • PVA glue and brush • craft knife • elastic • acrylic paints and paintbrush

1. Look at the pictures of *Triceratops* on p21. Sketch a mask design on the paper, making it slightly bigger than your face. Draw in the eyes, nose, horns and wavy neck frill.

2. With the plasticine, create a 3-D head shape on the board, following your sketch.

3. Build up the features on the face, plus the horns and neck frill using lumps of plasticine, making the mask 3-D.

4. Coat the plasticine mould with petroleum jelly. Tear up the newspaper and cover the mould with four layers of small, glued pieces. Leave to dry.

5. Remove the dried mask from the mould. Wipe off any excess petroleum jelly from the back.

6. Following your design, ask an adult to cut holes for the eyes with the knife (make sure they align with your eyes). Make two small holes in each side of the mask and thread elastic through to hold the mask on your head. Paint your mask.

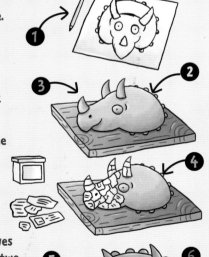

HOW TO USE
Wear your mask and practise scary roars in the mirror. Get your friends to make more masks for a dino-party!

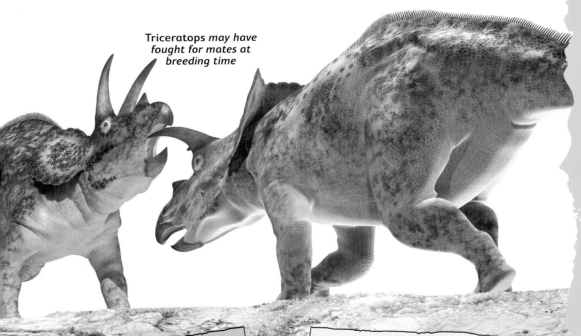

Triceratops may have fought for mates at breeding time

Because of their horns and armour, these dinosaurs were much heavier than others of the same length.

Triceratops
Length: 9 m
Weight: 10 tonnes

Rio jasaurus:
Length: 9 m
Weight: 2 tonnes

Edmontonia
Length: 7 m
Weight: 4 tonnes

Utahraptor
Length: 7 m
Weight: 0.4 tonnes

Minmi:
Length: 2 m
Weight: 500 kg

Oviraptor:
Length: 2 m
Weight: 30 kg

FRILLS AND HORNS

Triceratops was the biggest horn-faced dinosaur – 9 m long from its beak-like mouth to the tip of its tail. It had two one-metre-long eyebrow horns, a short nose horn, and a wide 'frill' of bone around its neck. It lived in North America 66 million years ago.

ARMOUR OUTSIDE

Euoplocephalus lived 75 million years ago in North America. It was 6 m long, and its body was low and wide. Almost every part of it had a hard covering of bone, including its face. Even the eyelids had tough shields, like bony shutters!

HEAVYWEIGHT CHEWERS

Ceratopsians and ankylosaurs were all plant-eaters. They snipped off leaves, buds and twigs with the beak-like front part of the mouth. It did not matter that they were slow-moving – their food did not run away!

21

HERDS AND HONKS

'Ornithopod' means 'bird-foot', and the ornithopod dinosaurs were named after their bird-like feet. Most were medium to large plant-eaters that walked on strong back legs. They include some of the best-known of all dinosaurs – and the noisiest!

▼ A big herd of *Iguanodon* would quickly eat all the plants in an area. So they probably moved long distances to find fresh food. This is called migration, which many animals, such as caribou and zebras, do today.

FOSSIL CLUES

Hundreds of fossil *Iguanodon* have been found, especially in Europe, so experts know a lot about this dinosaur. It lived 125 million years ago and grew to 10 m in length and 3 tonnes in weight. Some fossils include adults and young of various ages. They were probably a herd on the move when they suffered a disaster, such as a sudden flood or deadly fumes from a volcano.

Iguanodon could rear up on its back legs to get a better view of its surroundings

Air taken into nostrils to detect scents

PROTECTED BABIES

Fossil footprints show *Iguanodon* could run on two legs or bound along on four. They also show how youngsters remained in the middle of the group, protected from enemies by adults on the outside.

Dino-saurchestra!

Hum, honk, whistle or roar into these trumpet and didgeridoo mouth pieces to make dino noises!

SUPPLIES

To make the TRUMPET: large piece of coloured card • sticky tape • scissors

To make the DIDGERIDOO: large card tube (the bigger the better) • acrylic paint and paintbrush coloured craft foam • scissors • glue stick

To make the CASTANETS: thick card (8 cm x 20 cm) PVA glue and brush • two large buttons

HOW TO MAKE

1. To make the trumpet, roll the card into a funnel shape, with a small hole at one end. Firmly tape the card together along the join. Trim away the excess card around the large open end.

2. To make the didgeridoo, paint the large tube and leave to dry. Cut lots of scales from the craft foam. Use the glue stick to glue them all over the didgeridoo for decoration.

3. To make the castanets, fold the piece of card in half. Glue a button to the centre of each inside half with PVA and leave to dry.

HOW TO USE

Pinch the castanets between your fingers and thumb to get a clacking noise like dinosaurs approaching. Hum and roar into the trumpet and didgeridoo to make dino music!

IGUANODON KANGAROO?

Iguanodon fossils were pieced together into a complete skeleton in the 1880s. Scientists thought it stood on two back legs in a position called the 'kangaroo pose'.

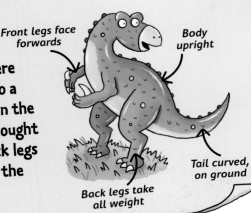

Front legs face forwards

Body upright

Back legs take all weight

Tail curved, on ground

Parasaurolophus:
Long curving crest 150 cm high

Corythosaurus:
Tall helmet-like crest 50 cm high

Lambeosaurus:
Tall oblong front crest 40 cm high with smaller tube behind

THE DUCKBILLS

The ornithopods called hadrosaurs, or duckbill dinosaurs, had a wide flat front to the mouth, like a duck's beak. Some also had strange-shaped head crests of hollow bone. Maybe they blew air through these crests to make sounds such as honks, hoots and bellows at breeding time, or to scare off enemies.

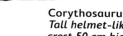

BUILT FOR SPEED

The fastest dinosaurs were slim and light, with a long neck and tail and long, powerful back legs to help them run fast. This body shape is similar to today's biggest bird, the fast-running ostrich, which is why these dinosaurs are called 'ostrich-dinosaurs' (ornithomimosaurs).

Beak-shaped mouth

Slim, lightweight body

DINO CHICKEN

Long tail for balance

One of the biggest ostrich-dinosaurs was *Gallimimus*, which lived 70 million years ago in Mongolia. It was 8 m long, stood 3 m high, and weighed over 200 kg. It's name means 'chicken mimic' – that's a very big chicken!

▶ *Gallimimus's long clawed fingers could dig up food such as worms and bugs.*

SUPER-QUICK DINO

Fastest of all dinosaurs may have been *Struthiomimus*, meaning 'ostrich mimic'. It was about the same height as an ostrich, with similar leg length.

How fast could it run? Maybe as fast as an ostrich...

▲ *Struthiomimus had strong muscles in its hips and legs, enabling it to take long, quick strides.*

Powerful leg muscles

EURASIA

N. AMERICA

AFRICA

S. AMERICA

INDIA

ANTARCTICA

AUSTRALIA

Dino world

The third part of the Mesozoic Era is called the Cretaceous Period. It lasted from 145–66 mya. During this period dinosaurs became bigger, faster and more varied than ever before.

Move the continents on your world map (p5) to their posi at the end of the Cretaceous Period. They are farther apar meaning dinosaurs evolved separately on huge 'islands'.

TRIASSIC	JURASSIC	CRETACEOUS	PALEOGENE	NEOGENE	QUATERN
252–201 mya	201–145 mya	145–66 mya	66–23 mya	23–2.6 mya	2.6 mya–

FOOD FOR THOUGHT

The ostrich eats almost any food, from hard seeds to leaves, grass and fruits, as well as bugs, worms and small animals. *Gallimimus* may have done the same, striding along to nip at plants and peck up creepy-crawlies.

MYSTERY ARMS

In 1965 a pair of huge dinosaur fossil arms and hands, 2.4 m long, were found in Mongolia – but no other body parts were with them. Named *Deinocheirus*, they looked like they belonged to a giant ostrich-dinosaur.

Long, bendy neck

▼ Recent finds show *Deinocheirus* was indeed a huge ostrich-dinosaur. It had a sail- or hump-back and was 13 m long, 5 m tall and weighed several tonnes – as big as *T rex!*

Game of survival!

Although *Gallimimus* was built for speed it might not win the survival game if it encountered too many dangers on the way.

SUPPLIES

50 cm sq thick white card • pencil • ruler • coloured felt-tip pens • A4 sheet of thin white card • four plastic bottle lids • sticky tack • dice • friends to play

HOW TO MAKE

1. Draw a grid on the card, with ten columns and ten rows.

2. Design some 'hazards' and 'rewards' into the grid (like 'Snakes and Ladders') that the dinosaurs might come across in their fight for survival, for example, meet a predator, outrun an enemy, escape up a tree, or get struck down by asteroids.

3. Pencil these onto the grid first to be sure of the positions. Number the squares 1 to 100, then colour in the board.

4. Draw some *Gallimimus* onto the thin card, copying the ones on p24. Make one for each player, no more than 5 cm long. Colour in and cut out.

5. Stick a lump of sticky tack to each bottle top and place a dinosaur on each one.

HOW TO USE

Each player must throw a six to start at square one. Take turns to move the dinosaurs around the board. The first dinosaur to reach 100 is the survivor!

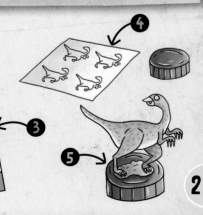

SCYTHES AND STONES

Among the last and strangest of all dinosaurs were the therizinosaurs, known as scythe-claws due to their enormous curved hand claws. They were related to fierce meat-eaters such as Tyrannosaurus, yet these amazing beasts had feathers and were probably plant-eaters. They are a real dino-puzzle.

Big claws!

Most dinosaurs had finger and toe claws, made from the same substance as our fingernails – keratin – but much bigger!

Utahraptor second toe claw 28 cm

Baryonyx thumb claw 30 cm

Therizinosaurus finger claw 95 cm

▼ The huge hand claws of therizinosaurs were almost one metre long. They may have been used to pull down or cut leaves from trees, which the dinosaur then ate with its spoon-shaped teeth.

SUPER SCYTHE

Scythe-claws appeared about 125 million years ago. The last and biggest was *Therizinosaurus*, which lived 70 million years ago in East Asia. At 10 m long and 5 tonnes in weight, it was almost as big as *Tyrannosaurus rex*.

Fossil hunt

Hide these fossilized claws in rocks and see if your friends can 'excavate' them in one piece.

SUPPLIES

pack of self-hardening modelling clay • large mi[xing] bowl • salt dough mix: 300g plain flour, 300g sa[lt] 200 ml water • spoon • old tray • sand/grit microwave oven • poster paints and paintbrush cocktail sticks • some adult help

STOMACH STONES

After swallowing, the plant food travelled into the dinosaur's crop (1.) where it was stored. The food then moved into the gizzard (2.) where gastroliths (swallowed stones) mashed it into an easily digested 'soup'.

FEATHERS

Most scythe-claw dinosaurs had a covering of fluffy feathers, but these were not designed for flight. Maybe the feathers kept in body warmth or had bright colours to impress mates.

HARD TO EAT

Tough, fibrous leaves, thick, woody stems, twigs and similar plant parts are very difficult to chew thoroughly so they can be digested properly. So many plant-eating dinosaurs used a secret weapon – they swallowed stones.

TO MAKE THE FOSSILS

1. Use the modelling clay to make some fossil shapes, such as the claws shown on p26. You could also make teeth and bone shapes.

2. Follow the instructions on the pack and leave the fossils to dry.

TO MAKE THE ROCKS (from the salt dough mix)

3. Place the salt and flour in the bowl and slowly stir in the water a little bit at a time – you may not need it all.

4. Knead the mixture with your hands until smooth. If the dough is too wet, add more flour. If it is too dry, add a little more water.

5. Take a handful of dough, and shape it into a rock around a fossil. Make sure the fossil is completely covered and hidden inside.

6. Sprinkle the sand/grit into the tray. Press the rocks in the sand they pick up a rough sandy texture all over.

7. To harden the rocks ask an adult to 'zap' them in a microwave. The exact cooking time will depend on the type of microwave but start with 3 minutes. If they are still wet then put them back for 20 seconds and repeat until dry.

8. Now the rocks are ready to paint. Choose colours to make them look really rocky. Use cocktail sticks to chip away the rock to find the fossils hidden inside!

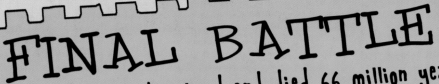

FINAL BATTLE

One dinosaur that lived and died 66 million years ago is more famous, and more studied, than almost any animal today. It was the global superstar *Tyrannosaurus*, or *T rex*. One of the last dinosaurs, it was also one of the biggest meat-eaters, and left amazing fossils for us to study.

KING OF THE MEAT-EATERS

At 12 m long and weighing 6 tonnes, *T rex* was the biggest land carnivore of its day. Its long, strong teeth were not particularly sharp – they were more suited to gristle-tearing and bone-crunching than slicing through flesh.

▼ Some fossils of *Triceratops* have tooth marks that match *T rex* teeth. But *Triceratops* was a big, tough dinosaur to tackle. Probably *T rex* attacked only the old, young, sick or injured, or scavenged on dead bodies.

BIG BONES, MIGHTY MUSCLES

Tyrannosaurus was certainly not lightweight in build. From its head, jaws and neck to its hips, legs and toes, it had thick, sturdy bones moved by powerful muscles.

SMILE PLEASE!

Fossils show that dinosaurs, like many reptiles today, continually grew new teeth to replace old ones that wore down or broke. So along the jaws were a mix of small new teeth and older big ones.

T rex puppet!

Make a *T rex* snarl and bite to show off his teeth!

SUPPLIES

pencil • A4 white card • tracing paper • colouring pencils or felt-tip pens • scissors • three split pins • two wooden dowels about 30 cm long • sticky tape

1. Copy the picture of the *T rex* adult on this page to A4 size.

2. Trace the *T rex* outline without the back legs and lower jaw. Transfer onto card, colour in and cut out.

3. Trace the outlines of the back legs and lower jaw and transfer them onto the card. Add a 3 cm tab where each piece will attach to the body. Colour in and cut out.

4. Attach the back legs to the body and the jaw to the neck with split pins, making sure the pieces move freely.

5. Tape the dowels to the back of the body and the lower jaw.

HOW TO USE

T rex is supported by the dowel attached to the body. The other dowel moves the jaw up and down. The legs will move when you shake the puppet!

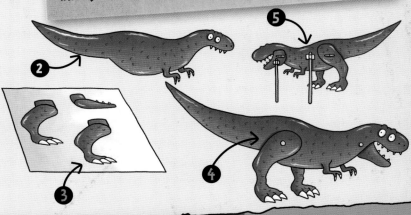

▲ *Tyrannosaurus* had tiny arms, probably hardly larger than yours, each with two mini-fingers. No one knows what they were for.

GROWTH SPURT

A baby *Tyrannosaurus* hatched from its egg was about 70 cm long. By 20 years it was a huge 12-m-monster.

T rex hatching

Most growth was during its teens, from ages 14–18.

T rex adult

What's in a name?

The first *T rex* fossils discovered in 1895 were thought to be of *Ornithomimus*.

Tyrannosaurus was officially named in 1905.

In 2000, the biggest *T rex* skeleton, 'Sue', went on display in Chicago.

NOT DEAD AT ALL

About 66 million years ago, disaster struck. Probably a massive space object — an asteroid or comet — crashed into Earth. The effects killed more than three-quarters of all plants and animals around the globe, including the great dinosaurs.

◄ Hundreds of volcanoes poured poison gases and suffocating ash into the air.

So many names

Dinosaurs have some weird names. Which one is your favourite?

First in alphabet list
– Aardonyx

Shortest names
– Mei, Kol, Zby

Longest name –
Micropachycephalosaurus

Most difficult to say
– Piatnitzkysaurus

Last in alphabet
list – Zupaysaurus

► Dead and dying dinosaurs were food for scavengers, but only for a short time.

BEFORE THE STRIKE

For a million years before the space rock hit, the world was already changing fast. Vast areas of volcanoes erupted in what is now India. Drifting continents reshaped seas. The climate altered rapidly.

ASTEROID WINTER

The space strike happened in the Gulf of Mexico, off the coast of Yucatan. It caused worldwide earthquakes, floods and more eruptions. Dust and fumes from volcanoes darkened the skies for years.

AFTER THE DISASTER

With the sun blotted out, plants died in the gloom. With their food gone, so did plant-eating animals, followed by the meat-eaters that preyed on them. The mass extinction affected land and sea.

ANCIENT BIRD

Confuciusornis was a prehistoric bird, and so a dinosaur. It had a toothless beak, a short bony tail, strong shoulder bones to anchor wing muscles, several kinds of feathers, and claws on its wings, like...

DINOSAURS LIVE ON

The modern view is that not all dinosaurs died out. Some small ones had already changed or evolved into birds, and many birds survived the great disaster. Today's birds are, in effect, living dinosaurs.

▲ *Tyrannosaurus* was one of the very last of the big dinosaurs.

Dino asteroid mobile

An asteroid strike meant disaster to all the great dinosaurs on Earth. Hang up this mobile to remember some of their amazing names!

SUPPLIES

this book • sheets of thin A4 card • pencil and tracing paper • colouring pencils or felt-tip pens • scissors one sheet of thick A4 card • small hole punch • string

HOW TO MAKE

1. Choose five favourite dinosaurs from this book. Draw or trace them onto the thin card. Colour them as you like and cut them out and. Write the correct name of each dinosaur on the back of each card. Make sure you get the spelling right!

2. Draw a large asteroid shape onto the thick card. Colour both sides then cut out. Punch five holes around the edge of the asteroid, plus one hole in the centre. If the hole punch doesn't reach, make this hole with a sharp pencil.

3. Punch a hole in the top of each dinosaur. Tie different lengths of string through each hole .

4. Now tie the other ends of the string to the asteroid.

5. Tie string through the centre of the asteroid and hang your mobile up.

INDEX

ACKNOWLEDGEMENTS

The publishers would like to thank the following artists who have contributed to this book:

Cover Florence Weiser (The Bright Agency)
Insides Peter Bull Art Studio, Stuart Jackson-Carter, and Chris Jevons (The Bright Agency)
All other artwork is from the Miles Kelly Artwork Bank

The publishers would like to thank the following sources for the use of their photographs:
t = top, c = centre, b = bottom, l = left, r = right, m = main
Alamy 30–31(m) Stocktrek Images, Inc., 31(under flap)

Amazon-Images **Corbis** 4 Mohamad Haghani/Stocktrek Images; 25(tr) Louie Psihoyos **Rex Features** 13(br) Jinyuan Liu **Shutterstock.com** 7(r) Jean-Michel Girard; 10(bl) Michael Rosskothen, (under flap) Michael Rosskothen; 14(bl) Andreas Meyer, (tr) Michael Rosskothen; 14–15(bg) Sergey Nivens, (t) Michael Rosskothen; 15(t) Catmando; 23(descending from cr) Jean-Michel Girard, Linda Bucklin; 24(l–r under flap) John Carnemolla, phugunfire, pandapaw, Eric Isselee; 28–29(m) Elenarts
Science Photo Library 26–27 Jose Antonio Peñas

Every effort has been made to acknowledge the source and copyright holder of each picture. Miles Kelly Publishing apologizes for any unintentional errors or omissions.